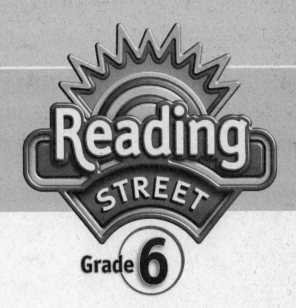

Grade **6**

Scott Foresman

Ten Important Sentences

D1568387

Editorial Offices: Glenview, Illinois • Parsippany, New Jersey • New York, New York
Sales Offices: Needham, Massachusetts • Duluth, Georgia • Glenview, Illinois
Coppell, Texas • Sacramento, California • Mesa, Arizona

ISBN: 0-328-16906-4

6 7 8 9 10 V034 11 10 09 08 07

Contents

Unit 1:   Loyalty and Respect

Unit 2:   Space and Time

Unit 3:   Challenges and Obstacles

Unit 4: Explorers, Pioneers, and Discoverers

Unit 5: Resources

Unit 6: Exploring Cultures

Why Are Sentences So Important?

The sentence is the basic means of written communication. In order to be literate and articulate, students need to master sentence power.

When students read, they get information from sentences. Sentences provide facts and details, opinions, clues about the sequence of events, and information to understand cause and effect relationships. Students cannot get such meaning from sounds or words alone. Readers use sentences to build meaning in context and to decide on a main idea. You can think of the steps to comprehension as an inverted triangle, illustrating that comprehension is built upon the understanding that sounds create words that are parts of sentences which make up a text.

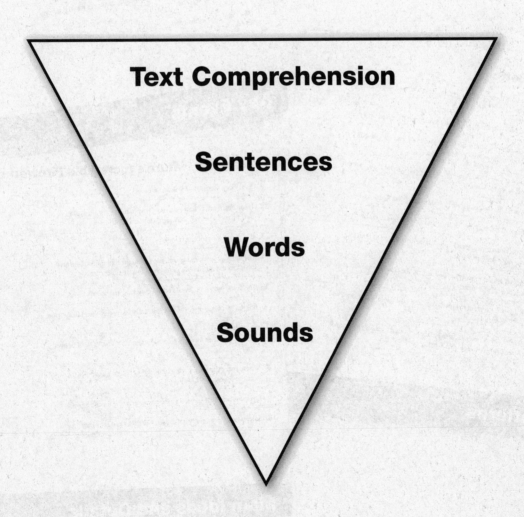

Text Comprehension

Sentences

Words

Sounds

In this booklet, Ten Important Sentences are provided for every selection in the Student Edition. Each sentence is logical and cohesive; each sentence provides a key idea from the selection. Together, the Ten Important Sentences help students make meaning in several ways. Depending on the genre, Ten Important Sentences can do any of the following:

- Present **key events** in a story or narrative nonfiction selection such as a biography or autobiography

- Give the stated **main ideas and details** in an essay or informational selection, or

- Demonstrate a predictable **pattern** in a selection, for example in a song, poem, or nonsense story

Gertrude Ederle

1. Gertrude Ederle was born on October 23, 1906.
2. She loved to swim.
3. By 1925 Trudy had set twenty-nine U.S. and world records.
4. She was determined to take on the ultimate challenge: the English Channel.
5. A newspaper editorial declared that Trudy wouldn't make it and that women must admit they would "remain forever the weaker sex."
6. She knew she would either swim the Channel or drown.
7. At about nine-forty at night, after more than fourteen hours in the water, Trudy's feet touched land.
8. She beat the men's record by almost two hours.
9. Reporters declared that the myth that women are the weaker sex was "shattered and shattered forever."
10. Gertrude Ederle had become a beacon of strength to girls and women everywhere.

Key Events

Tops & Bottoms

1. Once upon a time there lived a very lazy bear who had lots of money and lots of land.
2. So Hare and Mrs. Hare put their heads together and cooked up a plan.
3. "I'll do the hard work of planting and harvesting, and we can split the profit right down the middle," (said Hare).
4. Hare plucked off all the tops, tossed them into a pile for Bear, and put the bottoms aside for himself.
5. "But, Hare, all the best parts are in your half!" (said Bear).
6. Hare pulled off the bottoms for Bear and put the tops in his own pile.
7. "You've tricked me twice, and you owe me one season of both tops and bottoms!" (Bear growled).
8. Hare tugged off the roots at the bottom and the tassels at the top and put them in a pile for Bear.
9. "From now on I'll plant my own crops and take the tops, bottoms, and middles!" (Bear hollered).
10. Hare bought back his land with the profit from the crops, and he and Mrs. Hare opened a vegetable stand.

Patterns

Volcanoes: Nature's Incredible Fireworks

1. Every day somewhere volcanoes erupt.
2. If too much gas is trapped inside, part of the mountain may blow off, hurling rocks heavier than elephants for miles.
3. But not all volcanoes explode.
4. The answers lie deep beneath our feet in the four parts of the earth—the crust, the mantle, the outer core, and the inner core.
5. The crust, where we live, is covered by land and oceans.
6. It is several large pieces called plates that cover the planet like a giant jigsaw puzzle.
7. Where two plates meet, the force is so great that rocks bend or even break.
8. Where two plates meet, the mantle grows hotter, and volcanoes form near the edges.
9. Over thousands of years, a volcano may erupt again and again.
10. Scientists are learning what causes volcanoes and how they erupt.

Main Ideas and Details

How Ten Important Sentences Build Comprehension

Using and reusing *Ten Important Sentences* helps students build the skills they need for comprehension. *Ten Important Sentences* provides practical, selection-based instruction in these important skills:

• Recalling facts and details

• Finding and distinguishing between facts and opinions

• Arranging events in sequence

• Recognizing cause and effect relationships

• Identifying main idea and supporting details

You can help your students build their sentence power. Try these activities for building sentence power using *Ten Important Sentences*. The examples shown are from Grade 3. Match activities with other selections as you see fit.

Activity 1: Locate Sentences

1. Read the selection aloud to students or have students read all or parts of the selection silently.

2. Have students locate each of the Ten Important Sentences. (These will be those that tell the story or present the important ideas and details of the selection. The sentences on each master are in the correct order.) Discuss whether students agree with the choice of sentences. Which could they add or delete?

Activity 2: Distinguish Facts and Opinions

1. Read the selection aloud to students or have the students read all or parts of the selection silently. Discuss the selection, emphasizing sentences that are facts and sentences that are opinions.

2. Have students mark each of the Ten Important Sentences "F" for fact (something that can be proven) or "O" for opinion (something that a person believes or feels).

Me and Uncle Romie

1. Daddy thought it was a good time for me (James) to visit Uncle Romie and his wife, Aunt Nanette, up north in New York City. **F**

2. No, I wasn't sure about this visit at all. **O**

3. Home was like nothing I'd ever seen before. **F**

4. "Your uncle's working very hard, so we won't see much of him for a while" (said Aunt Nanette). **O**

5. My birthday was ruined. **F**

6. Looking at Uncle Romie's paintings, I could feel Harlem—its beat and bounce. **O**

7. "But the things we care about are pretty much the same" (said Uncle Romie). **O**

8. Uncle Romie held up two tickets to a baseball game! **F**

9. All these strangers talking to each other about their families and friends and special times, and all because of how my Uncle Romie's painting reminded them of things. **F**

10. And then I was off on a treasure hunt, collecting things that reminded me of Uncle Romie. **F**

Activity 3: Sequence Events

1. Read the selection aloud to students or have students read all or parts of the selection silently. Discuss the sequence of events, thoughts, or ideas in the selection.

2. Have students cut apart the Ten Important Sentences and mix the sentences in random order. Then have students order them correctly. (Note: Students can work with the sentences numbered or not, as you wish.)

Sequence
We all got together to build a church and a school.
Now this was a real boom town!

Activity 4: Link Cause and Effect

1. Read the selection aloud to students or have students read all or parts of the selection silently. Talk about events in the story and what causes them to happen.

2. Have students look at the Ten Important Sentences and find one or more pairs of sentences in which one sentence tells what happens and the other tells why it happens.

Cause
"There is more snow here than at home in England," said William.

Effect
He built a new roof with a very steep pitch and replaced the shingles.

Activity 5: Determine Main Idea

1. After reading, focus on the selection and talk with students about the big ideas.

2. Have students locate the sentences that provide the five elements of the main idea: who? did what? where? when? and why? Help students as they write the answers to these important questions in one sentence of their own.

Every day somewhere volcanoes erupt.

Notice that over time, students listen, manipulate sentences, and draw conclusions as they work toward comprehending what they have read. Using the Ten Important Sentences frees you from creating worksheets and lets you concentrate on helping students read and write with confidence.

The Main Idea Glove

U se the main idea glove to talk about the five elements of main idea. Duplicate this outline for each child or post it in your classroom. Your student will have the main idea right at hand!

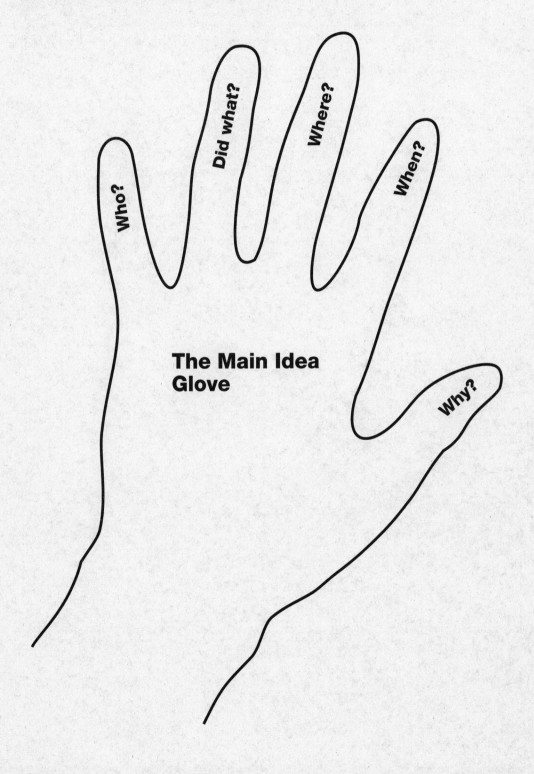

The Main Idea Glove

Name _____

Old Yeller

1. From the time he'd (Little Arliss) grown up big enough to get out of the cabin, he'd made a practice of trying to catch and keep every living thing that ran, flew, jumped, or crawled.

2. Then, after the yeller dog came, Little Arliss started catching even bigger game.

3. I told Mama then, I said: "Mama, that old yeller dog is going to make the biggest liar in Texas out of Little Arliss."

4. I think Mama had let him tell so many big yarns about his catching live game that he'd begun to believe them himself.

5. This time I knew Little Arliss was in real trouble.

6. He (Little Arliss) was lying half in and half out of the water, holding onto the hind leg of a little black bear cub no bigger than a small coon.

7. Then, just as the bear went lunging up the creek bank toward Little Arliss and her cub, a flash of yellow came streaking out of the brush.

8. She'd knock him so far that it didn't look like he could possibly get back there before she charged again, but he always did.

9. I didn't see it, of course, but Mama said that the minute Old Yeller saw we were all in the clear and out of danger, he threw the fight to that she bear and lit out for the house.

10. The way he acted, you might have thought that bear fight hadn't been anything more than a rowdy romp that we'd all taken part in for the fun of it.

© Pearson Education 6

Mother Fletcher's Gift

----

1. "I am Mother Fletcher and you can call for an ambulance," (said Mother Fletcher).

----

2. O'Brien talked to her now and again when he saw her on the street, and started writing down everything she said, trying to piece together enough information to determine her true age.

----

3. The struggle and hassles of Harlem were not what he wanted to bring home with him.

----

4. "The place she (Mother Fletcher) lives in isn't very nice, and Daddy would rather not spend his Christmas in that kind of a neighborhood," (said Bill).

----

5. "We're going to Mother Fletcher's for dinner," Meaghan said brightly.

----

6. "But it's good for you to see we have holidays here too," (said Mother Fletcher).

----

7. "You don't survive, and that's what I been doing all these years, you don't survive sitting around expecting folks to act right," (said Mother Fletcher).

----

8. "But you got to be ready when they do act right because that's what makes the surviving worth surviving," (said Mother Fletcher).

----

9. This is a story about how a policeman's young family brought a few hours of happiness to an old woman.

----

10. Or perhaps it's about how an old woman taught a young family something about sharing.

Viva New Jersey

1. All Lucinda had were her memories—and now this dog, whom she untied from the tree.

2. Pets were not allowed in her building, and her family could be evicted.

3. Knowing that her parents would arrive any moment, Lucinda gathered up the dog, covering him with her coat, and carried him down nine flights to the basement.

4. An outline of a plan was taking shape in her mind.

5. The building had been pitched into darkness.

6. Lucinda looked frantically for the dog, but he was gone.

7. Lucinda didn't plan it, but she found herself in front of Ashley's house minutes later.

8. For the first time since leaving her homeland, she (Lucinda) felt somewhat at peace with herself.

9. Chauncey was back!

10. She (Lucinda) reached Ashley's doorstep just as the first fire engine turned the corner.

Saving the Rain Forests

1. A rain forest is a special kind of forest that grows in warm, wet places.

2. Because of this, scientists say rain forests have a high biodiversity (variety of living things).

3. Removing rain forests cuts down the amount of oxygen in the air, threatening the lives of many plants and animals.

4. Half the world's rain forests have been destroyed to provide timber or farmland.

5. Mining, industrial development, and the building of large dams all damage the rain forests too.

6. The rain forest is like a huge sponge.

7. If the trees are cleared away, there are no roots to hold the soil.

8. With fewer trees, rainwater drains away quickly.

9. Many forest plants could be the source of new medicines or foods.

10. The challenge for the future is finding ways for people to live in rain forests, find sufficient food in them, earn a living from them, and look after them, all at the same time.

When Crowbar Came

----

1. A violent windstorm had knocked bird and nest out of a tree.

----

2. At the end of the day we had a pet crow.

----

3. He (Crowbar) cuddled against Luke, begged until Craig petted his head and chin, and dropped spoons and forks off the kitchen table until someone talked to him.

----

4. He (Crowbar) did concede one thing to his heredity, however: He slept in the apple tree outside the kitchen window.

----

5. I read that crows are hard to study because they're so smart.

----

6. Of course: While soaring above the trees, he (Crowbar) had spotted the kids and their food and shiny money.

----

7. He (Crowbar) looked around and then deposited his money in the bank's rainspout.

----

8. "We have a lot to learn (about crows)," (said Mrs. Tee Van).

----

9. I had never had a massive gang of crows come to abduct a pet.

----

10. Despite our tears, it was a beautiful ending to a wild-pet story.

The Universe

1. The sun, the closest star to us, is over four hundred times farther away from us than the moon is—about ninety-three million miles.

2. We measure the distance to the stars in light-years: the distance that light travels in one year, which is close to six *trillion* miles.

3. But in recent years, scientists using new instruments began to observe what looked like other solar systems in the making.

4. Still, we have discovered more planets around distant stars than in our own solar system.

5. Our sun is just one of about two hundred billion stars in the Milky Way galaxy, a vast spiral of stars about one hundred thousand light-years across.

6. The central galaxy is much more crowded than our lonely part of space.

7. Many galaxies in space are so distant that their light fades out before it reaches the Earth, and they can only be seen with radio telescopes.

8. Scientists think that there are at least one hundred billion galaxies in the universe, and each galaxy contains about one hundred billion stars.

9. Looking at distant galaxies in the universe with a telescope is like using a time machine to peer into the past.

10. But with the Hubble Space Telescope and other new methods of gathering information, we are just at the beginning of a golden age of discovery.

Dinosaur Ghosts

1. Hundreds of *Coelophysis* (SEEL-oh-FIE-sis) dinosaurs perished together here, in a tangle of necks, tails, arms, and legs.

2. After studying the *Coelophysis* bones to learn what these dinosaurs were like when they were alive, the scientists turned their attention to the positions of the bones in the ground.

3. Looking closely at the skeletons, paleontologists could see that none of the bones of any of the dinosaurs or other animals seemed to be cracked from drying a long time in the sun.

4. We can test these scientific suggestions, or hypotheses, by comparing them with the evidence found in the bones and the rocks around them.

5. If the dinosaurs *had* been trapped in mud, as they struggled their heavier legs would be buried more deeply than their arms and heads, and their bodies would be upright.

6. If there were even traces of volcanic ash, under the microscope the rocks would have a few tiny smashed bubbles of the mineral silica.

7. The dinosaurs aren't scattered over a large area, as they would be if they collapsed, one by one, from hunger.

8. Poison that would kill dinosaurs would probably make the water unfit for other animals too—especially ones that had to live *in* the water.

9. Why were these dinosaurs arranged differently from the rest?

10. The real picture may be a combination of two suggestions—a drought *and* a flood.

A Week in the 1800s

1. A group of modern kids stepped back into the 1800s at Kings Landing Historical Settlement in New Brunswick, Canada.

2. Kings Landing is a special kind of museum, a village of nineteenth-century farms, homes, shops, and mills that bring history to life.

3. Once their bonnets were tied and suspenders buttoned, the kids learned about the manners that went along with their nineteenth-century clothing.

4. Looking at a bedroom with a bed, a dresser, and not much else, Brandon M. realized that people back then didn't have as many things as we do today.

5. Imagine preparing three meals a day, when cooking included making every loaf of bread and hunk of cheese.

6. The girls had known before that nineteenth-century women didn't have as many choices and rights.

7. But they (the girls) didn't like being in that position themselves.

8. In the nineteenth century, a boy often couldn't choose the work he'd do as a grown-up.

9. In the nineteenth century, farming was more a way of life than a business.

10. Suddenly they valued parts of the twentieth century they had taken for granted because they had never known life without them.

Good-bye to the Moon

1. Mother had been dead for five years, and I, Kepler Masterman, son of Moon Governor, was actually going to Earth myself.

2. But it was only twelve or thirteen times a year, and there was something special about the sunlight creeping so slowly across the surface of Moon, striking the peaks of the Apennines, sending shadows chasing across the Sinus Aestium, each Earth-day a little closer, until finally the two long weeks of night were over, and we were bathed in sunlight again.

3. Letter rates to Earth were crippling—so was the cost of everything that had to make the 240,000-mile haul.

4. Now that the hydroponic gardens were going, we didn't have to pay for our oxygen any more.

5. I had grown up thinking water was the most precious stuff in the Universe.

6. Half a world made of water, and yet they had charged us for every single cup.

7. I had not realized until this moment what my birthright of one-sixth Earth weight was going to mean when I tried to return "home."

8. "I anticipate that it may take as long as six months to settle our differences, though of course we could strike it lucky. . . " (said the Governor).

9. It was strange being outdoors without a space-suit, scary but exciting.

10. I lay back and thought of the pyramids and the Taj Mahal, the temples of Angkor Wat, and the mysterious jungle buildings of the Incas.

Egypt

1. The pharaoh and his family were at the top rung of Egyptian society.

2. They (the pharaoh and his family) lived in great luxury.

3. Artisans, merchants, and engineers made up the middle class.

4. The common people were farmers, laborers, and soldiers.

5. Ancient paintings and artifacts show how much the Egyptians loved games.

6. The new year began with the flooding of the Nile in July.

7. In November, as the waters receded, *peret*—the plowing and planting season—began.

8. The floodwaters left a deposit of silt that fertilized the fields and produced abundant crops.

9. Egyptians were writing with picture symbols called hieroglyphs as early as 3000 B.C.

10. To make sure they would have eternal life, pharaohs built fabulous tombs for themselves.

Hatchet

1. A porcupine had stumbled into his shelter and when he (Brian) had kicked it, the thing had slapped him with its tail of quills.

2. I can't take it this way, alone with no fire and in the dark, and next time it might be something worse, maybe a bear, and it wouldn't be just quills in the leg, it would be worse.

3. He did not know how long it took, but later he looked back on this time of crying in the corner of the dark cave and thought of it as when he learned the most important rule of survival, which was that feeling sorry for yourself didn't work.

4. The nick wasn't large, but the hatchet was important to him, was his only tool, and he should not have thrown it.

5. When he threw the hatchet at the porcupine in the cave and missed and hit the stone wall it had showered sparks, a golden shower of sparks in the dark, as golden with fire as the sun was now.

6. Brian found it was a long way from sparks to fire.

7. He pulled and twisted bits off the trees, packing them in one hand while he picked them with the other, picking and gathering until he had a wad close to the size of a baseball.

8. He needed to add air.

9. When the small wood was going well he went out and found larger wood and did not relax until that was going.

10. A friend and a guard from a tiny spark.

Name _____

When Marian Sang

1. Church folks started whispering and followed with out-and-out talking about Marian's remarkable gift.

2. Audiences heard not only words, but feelings too: spirited worship, tender affection, and nothing short of joy.

3. For her, music was serious business, and more than anything, she hoped to someday go to music school.

4. Marian knew about prejudice.

5. But she could not understand how anyone who was surrounded by the spirit and beauty of music could be so narrow-minded.

6. Many times, she was welcomed enthusiastically by her audiences, and then could not get a hotel room because she was Negro.

7. Audiences applauded in London, cheered in Paris, and pounded on the stage for encores in Russia.

8. She *could* go anywhere and sing for anyone. . . until she came home to the United States.

9. Washington, D.C., was a boiling pot about to spill over.

10. Examining her heart, Marian realized that although she was a singer first and foremost, she also had become a symbol to her people and she wanted to make it easier for those who would follow her.

Name _____

Learning to Swim

1. This summer, I thought, I would work harder and learn to swim as smoothly and gracefully as my mother.

2. By mid-August, in both the front crawl and the breaststroke, I could swim easily downstream—all the way to the rock that marked the end of the swimming area.

3. That summer, during the third week of August, two of my uncles, their wives, and my mother decided to take a trip to the Sea of Japan for the weekend, bringing my brother, our cousins, and me.

4. I don't know how long we were riding the waves before I noticed that my mother and I hadn't seen anyone for a long time.

5. If it weren't for me, I thought, she could easily swim back to the shore.

6. The waves had been pushing us sideways, toward the rocks, as well as farther from the shore.

7. That piece of land was our last chance.

8. The waves we had been fighting were suddenly helping us.

9. The way she talked about it, our experience in the Sea of Japan was a great adventure that proved my courage: If I could swim well enough not to drown in a place where a fisherman had died in a rip tide, then I never again had to worry about drowning.

10. The other side of the pool didn't look nearly as far away as the shore had from the sea the day I had almost drowned.

© Pearson Education 6

Ten Important Sentences • *Unit 3, Week 3* 13

Name _____

Juan Verdades

1. Finally don Arturo declared loudly, "I'll bet you whatever you want that within two weeks at the most I'll make this Juan Verdades tell you a lie."

2. That night don Arturo and his daughter made up a plan.

3. Each morning she did the same thing, and Juan Verdades began to fall in love with Araceli, which was just what the girl and her father expected.

4. What Araceli hadn't expected was that she began to fall in love with Juan Verdades too and looked forward to getting up early every morning just to be alone with him.

5. Araceli continued to work on the plan she and her father had made—but she now had a plan of her own as well.

6. Each day they repeated the conversation.

7. Finally, just the day before the two weeks of the bet would have ended, the foreman gave in.

8. "Some fool picked your apples and gave them away," (Juan replied).

9. He (don Ignacio) glanced toward the window where Araceli was watching and went on: "Sign it over to don Juan Verdades."

10. "Don Juan Verdades," he said, "I'll be proud to have such an honest man for a son-in-law."

Elizabeth Blackwell

1. **NARRATOR TWO** A well brought up lady cannot be a doctor.

2. **ELIZABETH** Times won't change unless we make them change!

3. **DEAN SNYDER** If we admit a woman, our enrollment will decline.

4. **DR. BLOT** Unfortunately, you have the same disease as the baby you were treating.

5. **ELIZABETH** If I can't be a surgeon, Anna, I will be a doctor!

6. **NARRATOR THREE** No hospital wanted to hire her.

7. **NARRATOR TWO** Finally she opened a clinic in the immigrant slums of New York City.

8. **ELIZABETH** If the body can't breathe, if the body isn't clean, if the body is malnourished, it cannot get well!

9. **NARRATOR ONE** She worked around the clock seeing patients, sometimes the only figure on a darkened street hurrying through the night to save someone.

10. **ELIZABETH** Because the real sickness is prejudice!

Into the Ice

1. Nansen had a breathtaking proposal: he would sail a ship directly into the ice pack off Siberia, deliberately let it be frozen in, and drift with the ice across the top of the world, penetrating the heart of the Arctic.

2. The scientific expedition was a triumphant success, and Nansen and Johansen had gone farther north than anyone had before.

3. Now the race to the North Pole was on.

4. Another daring attempt was made the very next year—a flight to the Pole in a balloon.

5. We know what happened only because thirty-three years later their frozen remains were found, along with Andrée's journal and another eerie relic—undeveloped images of the doomed expedition that were still in their camera.

6. Physically the North Pole is nothing more than a theoretical point on the Earth's surface—but reaching it came to symbolize mankind's mastery of the entire planet—and a landmark human achievement.

7. Peary came home to the stunning news that Dr. Cook had already returned, claiming to have reached the North Pole on April 21, 1908, a year before Peary.

8. In recent years, historical researchers have determined that neither man actually stepped foot on the northernmost point of the globe.

9. The classic era of Arctic exploration ended with Peary.

10. Arctic flights are great achievements, but they are achievements of technology, somehow different from crossing nearly five hundred miles of shifting ice by dog sledge and then returning.

The Chimpanzees I Love

1. The more we have learned about chimpanzees, the clearer it is that they have brains very like ours and can, in fact, do many things that we used to think only humans could do.

2. So the chimps have their own primitive culture.

3. They (chimps) have excellent memories—after eleven years' separation, a female named Washoe recognized the two humans who had bought her up.

4. A chimp can plan what he or she is going to do.

5. Chimpanzees can be taught to do many of the things that we do, such as riding bicycles and sewing.

6. Chimps can learn 300 signs or more.

7. Unfortunately chimpanzees, so like us in many ways, are often very badly treated in many captive situations.

8. Chimpanzees live in the forested areas of west and central Africa.

9. Like the other African great apes, the gorillas and bonobos, they are disappearing very fast.

10. There are many people and organizations trying to help protect chimpanzees and their forests, but the problems are very hard to solve.

Black Frontiers

1. When the Civil War ended, men and women who had been slaves waited to see what freedom would bring.

2. These sharecroppers soon found they were perpetually in debt.

3. Homesteading was not easy for black or white settlers.

4. In the early days of settlement, there were few black families homesteading.

5. But black pioneer families held on, and in sticking it out, they made the way easier for those who came after.

6. By 1879 an exodus of black families out of the Old South began, and before long, there were eight hundred homesteaders in the new Kansas communities of Dunlap and Nicodemus.

7. The Buffalo Soldiers helped to bring law and order to regions where ranchers fought with farmers, where Indian tribes warred with each other and with settlers, and where bandits threatened to overrun small towns.

8. It would be wrong to suggest that the frontier was without prejudice.

9. But on those lonely, dangerous, and beautiful lands we call the frontier, black pioneers built new lives.

10. West of the Mississippi, between 1850 and 1900, there were some ten thousand African American exodusters, homesteaders, and sod busters.

Space Cadets

----

1. **CAPTAIN** We've entered a new solar system, 73 light years from Earth.

----

2. **ENSIGN** We're detecting seven planets: four R-class planets, two L-class, and an M-class.

----

3. **FIRST OFFICER** Actually, Sir, M-class planets are the most hospitable for carbon-based life forms.

----

4. **FIRST OFFICER** My computers show the atmosphere to be breathable, and I am picking up signs of several types of life forms on the planet's surface.

----

5. **CAPTAIN** As we all know, our mission is to make first contact.

----

6. **CAPTAIN** I want you to beam down to the planet below, seek out the first life forms you find, and make contact.

----

7. **TOM** An alien.

----

8. **FIRST OFFICER** First Officer to Ept. Three to beam up—and make it fast.

----

9. **OG** Why do you suppose they kept trying to talk to Bessie?

----

10. **OG** There is no intelligent life out there.

Inventing the Future

1. When he was 22 years old, Edison received his first patent.

2. The experience taught him a valuable lesson: Never again would he invent something that people didn't want to buy.

3. By the age of 23, Edison had earned a reputation as one of the best electrical inventors in the country, which helped him attract more financial backers.

4. In Newark, Edison first developed the method of team inventing that would characterize the rest of his career.

5. Edison was not discouraged when things went wrong.

6. If the human voice could travel over wires, he reasoned, then there should be a way to record the sound so that it could be listened to later.

7. He soon set it aside, however, to concentrate on the greatest challenge of his career—the development of an electric lighting system that could be used in homes and businesses.

8. Confident of Edison's genius, several rich investors established the Edison Electric Light Company to cover his expenses.

9. Finally his persistence was rewarded.

10. Over the next two years, Edison and his crew worked feverishly to invent the many other devices besides the light bulb that were needed to get a full lighting system up and running.

The View from Saturday

1. I (Noah) peeled off the Post-it note containing my list and stuck it on the wall in front of my desk, and then, as my mother had commanded, I thought again.

2. It all started when Margaret Draper and Izzy Diamondstein decided to get married, and the citizens of Century Village called a meeting in the clubhouse to organize the wedding.

3. I was doing a wonderful job until Thomas Stearns, called T.S., Tillie's cat, pounced into my lap, and I jumped up and spilled the ink, and the cat walked through the spilled ink and onto a couple of the invitations I was addressing.

4. On the Post-it I wrote (in faultless calligraphy): Bring this specially marked invitation to the wedding and receive a surprise gift.

5. Unfortunately, he (Allen Diamondstein) didn't see the wagon handle, so he tripped on it, slid on the wet concrete, fell in the puddle of melted ice, and, unfortunately, toppled the wedding cake.

6. Since I had promised to be best man, not having a tux was a problem.

7. Bella had a supply of fabric paints, and within two hours, we had painted a T-shirt that looked like a tuxedo and a red bow tie.

8. I did an excellent job of being best man even though when I was under the chupah, I was under a lot of pressure trying to think of surprises for the cat's-paw invitations.

9. It would mean giving up things I loved, but I had to do it.

10. In that way each of my gifts kept on giving.

Name _____

Harvesting Hope

----

1. Until Cesar Chavez was ten, every summer night was like a fiesta.

----

2. Without water for the crops, the Chavez family couldn't make money to pay its bills.

----

3. Now he (Cesar) and his family were migrants—working on other people's farms, crisscrossing California, picking whatever fruits and vegetables were in season.

----

4. As he worked, it disturbed him that landowners treated their workers more like farm tools than human beings.

----

5. And in his early twenties, he decided to dedicate the rest of his life to fighting for change.

----

6. In a fight for justice, he told everyone, truth was a better weapon than violence.

----

7. Instead, he organized a march—a march of more than three hundred miles.

----

8. Now students, public officials, religious leaders, and citizens from everywhere offered help.

----

9. From the steps of the state capitol building, the joyous announcement was made to the public: Cesar Chavez had just signed the first contract for farmworkers in American history.

----

10. Some of the wealthiest people in the country had been forced to recognize some of the poorest as human beings.

Name _____

River to the Sky

1. "Oh, how I wish I could go to the sky," said the River, sighing as it fell asleep.

2. Away into the sky the wind carried the whisper.

3. Gazelle, who happened to be taking a drink just then, sprang up and ran to Elephant and said, "The Sun is going to take the great River up to the sky, and she says she'll never come back here again!"

4. That started the exodus, and animals wandered in all directions.

5. It (the Sun) sent its hottest rays to heat the River, and slowly, oh so slowly you could not see what was happening, the River started to lift in particles too tiny for the eye to see.

6. Then the tiny particles of the River huddled together and formed white fluffy clouds of all sizes.

7. Now, pushing and shoving is about the only thing that the gentle River would not stand.

8. They carried the clouds high and made them feel colder, and as the clouds huddled together they grew heavy and began to fall as rain.

9. It rained and rained everywhere but never in the place where the River once lived.

10. If any of the drops ventured anywhere near that place, the Sun bore down on them and sent them back into the sky.

Gold

----

1. Glistening bright yellow, gold is a heavy metal that is treasured in every country of the world.

----

2. Gold is special because its luster never fades.

----

3. Gold is 19.3 times denser than water and three times denser than iron.

----

4. Gold is extremely rare, which is one of the many reasons why we value it so highly.

----

5. The leading areas for goldmining include South Africa, Russia, the United States, Canada, Australia, Brazil, and China.

----

6. The oceans, which cover about three-quarters of Earth's surface, contain a much higher proportion of gold than the land.

----

7. Cities have been founded and expeditions and wars started by people scrabbling for more of this precious metal.

----

8. Gold objects never corrode.

----

9. Pure gold is extremely malleable, which means that it is soft enough to bend or beat into many different shapes.

----

10. Compared to most metals, gold has atoms that are bonded together very loosely.

The House of Wisdom

1. The House of Wisdom became like a beacon, drawing to itself a thousand scholars from all over the world.

2. Here in the House of Wisdom, a boy named Ishaq lived with his father and his mother.

3. "That searching is the great adventure; it is the fire in our hearts," (said Hunayn).

4. Aristotle would have looked at these same stars a thousand years ago.

5. And so, many mornings Ishaq sat with his books, reading the ancient Greek words one at a time, then writing them in Arabic, slowly.

6. But still he (Ishaq) did not feel the fire.

7. And then one day the Caliph chose Ishaq to lead an expedition to search for books.

8. Everything he (Ishaq) saw and heard and felt was new and strange, but for the rising of the sun each day and the canopy of stars at night.

9. It seemed to him that the lights of the scholars' lanterns were like new stars that had come close to Earth, and that the glow of those lanterns might reach to the darkness of the land he had seen.

10. He (Ishaq) thought of scholars through time reading and copying and translating and saving what Aristotle had written, an unbroken chain leading all the way to Baghdad, all the way to Ishaq, a thousand years later.

Don Quixote and the Windmills

1. Señor Quexada longed to live in days gone by, when gallant knights battled for the honor of ladies fair.

2. He read all day and far into the night, until his mind snapped.

3. "I am the renowned knight and champion Don Quixote de la Mancha," (said Señor Quexada).

4. One moonless night, while everyone in town lay asleep, Don Quixote and Sancho set forth.

5. He (Don Quixote) galloped across the plain to do battle with the windmills.

6. His lance pierced the canvas sail and became tangled in the ropes.

7. The faithful squire (Sancho) found himself pulled off his donkey and carried aloft with his master.

8. "At the last moment, he (the wizard Frestón)transformed the giants into windmills to deprive me of the glorious victory that was rightfully mine," (said Don Quixote).

9. "Our names and the stories of our matchless deeds will resound through the ages," (said Don Quixote).

10. Sancho mounted his donkey and went trotting after Rocinante, vowing to follow Don Quixote wherever fortune's winds might carry him.

Ancient Greece

1. The modern Olympics are one of many traditions developed in Greece.

2. Greek ideas are found in today's governments, art, architecture, and literature.

3. They are also seen in science, drama, and athletics.

4. Each city-state ruled itself and had its own customs.

5. After the Persian Wars, Athens entered its Golden Age.

6. For 27 years, Athens and Sparta and their allies fought in the Peloponnesian War.

7. Alexander founded many military colonies in the lands he conquered.

8. After conquering the Greeks, the Roman Empire grew.

9. Greece has influenced many modern governments.

10. Every day, people take part in activities invented by the ancient Greeks.

The All-American Slurp

1. We had emigrated to this country from China, and during our early days here we had a hard time with American table manners.

2. Mr. and Mrs. Gleason, their daughter Meg, who was my friend, and their neighbors, the Badels—they were all staring at us as we busily pulled the strings of our celery.

3. Mrs. Gleason bent down and whispered to us, "This is a buffet dinner."

4. The Gleasons' dinner party wasn't so different from a Chinese meal after all.

5. Then came our dinner at the Lakeview restaurant.

6. As any respectable Chinese knows, the correct way to eat your soup is to slurp.

7. And in the silence, our family's consumption of soup suddenly seemed unnaturally loud.

8. All of us, our family and the Chinese guests, stopped eating to watch the activities of the Gleasons.

9. She frowned and shook her head slightly, and I understood the message: the Gleasons were not used to Chinese ways, and they were just coping the best they could.

10. "All Americans slurp," (said Meg).

The Aztec News

1. Ahead of me, I can see our army's finest warriors, the Eagles and the Jaguars, rounding up captives to be sent back to our city for sacrifice.

2. Today, the murderous invaders lie dead in the thousands, many of them still clinging greedily to their stolen gold.

3. As the enemy fled, our warriors took to their canoes.

4. Of course, there are many benefits to being a noble.

5. But there's a downside to everything, of course.

6. Your first sight of our glorious island city will take your breath away—if, that is, you have any left after the long climb over the mountains that surround Lake Texcoco!

7. Covering nearly 6 square miles, our city (Tenochtitlán) is home to more than 250,000 people.

8. Most traders will accept a variety of goods in exchange for their wares, but you might find it easier to take along some cocoa beans or pieces of copper instead.

9. But when I was a young warrior marching across the empire with the army, I often saw these merchants trading in faraway cities.

10. And I began to realize that it's the pochtecas who help to make our city so rich.

Name _____

Where Opportunity Awaits

- -

1. The Thomases were part of the first Great Migration—the collective journeys of a half-million black southerners to northern cities between 1916 and 1919.

- -

2. By 1918, migration chains that linked South to North enabled thousands of southerners to choose destinations where they had friends or relatives to offer a welcoming hand.

- -

3. In most cases, these patterns conformed largely to patterns established by railroad routes.

- -

4. Because these migrants arrived during a wartime housing shortage, most encountered difficulty finding a place to live.

- -

5. Hence, African Americans spent a very high percentage of their income on shelter.

- -

6. During World War I and at times during the 1920s, black newcomers found places to work in northern cities much more easily than they found places to live.

- -

7. It was far more difficult for many migrants from the South to adapt to a different approach to time.

- -

8. In the rural South, just as in other agricultural societies, the calendar and the weather determined the work pace.

- -

9. What did not require adjustment, however, was hard work.

- -

10. The difference for most migrants—the reason why most not only stayed but also encouraged their friends and relatives to join them—was that the hard work produced rewards during the war years and in the 1920s.

- -